Gondor Writing Centre Creative Writing Guide
Book 1
Turning an idea into a story

Creative Writing Guide
Book 1
Turning an idea into a story.

© Copyright Elaine Ouston, Australia 2021

Published by

Morris Publishing Australia

http://morrispublishingaustralia.com

ISBN: 978-0-6488782-2-3

All rights reserved. No part of this publication may be reproduced, stored in a retrieval system, or transmitted, in any form or by means, electronic, mechanical, photocopying, recording or otherwise, without the prior written permission of the copyright holder.

CONTENTS:

Chapter One – Nine Building Blocks of Story — 1

Chapter Two – Developing Strong Characters — 11

Chapter Three – Establishing Point of View — 17

Chapter Four – Creating the Best Setting — 25

Character Questionnaire — 29

Introduction:

Many people tell me they are going to write a book one day and the idea they have will make it a best seller. Now it is great to have that kind of confidence, but when I ask them what knowledge and experience they have as a writer, they say things like, "I was top of my class in English."

If only it was that simple. There is more to writing a best seller than knowing basic English. Having been through the journey from having ideas to turning them into popular books for children, I can tell you it is not that easy.

To me, saying you can write a best-seller without learning about **the craft of story creation** is like saying you are going to do brain surgery without going to medical school.

50% of writing a great work of fiction is imagination and 50% is technical skill on how to build a great story, but these skills can be learned.

Like all professions, to be the best at what you do, you have to work at it. Many people can tell a story, but if it doesn't excite and intrigue the readers on the first page they won't read on.

These skills are needed whatever you are writing – short story, picture book, chapter books for children, poems, memoirs, novels, etc.

This book and the ones that follow will help you learn those skills.

Chapter One

BUILDING BLOCKS OF STORY

I am often asked where writers get ideas for stories. Some tell me they come to them in a dream, others from meeting an interesting character, some from reading or listening to a real-life story, learning about something new, or just from a passion for a subject. For many fiction writers, the main character pops into their mind and demands their story be told. Mine usually come from learning something new and deciding to write a story about it.

There are many forms of story: short stories, novels, novellas, poems and more. And many genres; memoir, non-fiction, contemporary fiction, historic, romantic, fantasy, humour, thriller, crime etc. It doesn't matter what you are writing, the information that you will be given, will help you develop your story.

This guide will introduce you to the building blocks of a great story. And I encourage you to use your idea to do the exercises that are a part of the lesson.

You need to have each one of these building blocks clear in your mind before you start writing. In this book, I can only touch on each of the subjects I will cover. The guides that follow will cover them in more detail.

Once you have an idea, you have to come up with the best way to tell the story. A good story follows a set pattern or a story arc.

Following are the 9 building blocks of story. But before we get to them, we need to know who the main character is.

Character: Every story needs a main character; this is the person whose story you will tell. Depending on the type of story and the audience, this can of course be an animal or an imaginary creature.

Many people develop their character first and make the mistake of starting their story with a whole chapter on the character, where he lives, works, what he looks like etc. You will lose your reader before they get to the story if you do this.

While is vital for **you** to know all of those things and more about your character, all of those details should be revealed to the reader through the story. While I usually have a character in mind before I start planning, I have learnt not to develop him/her too much before the story is clear in my mind. I believe the character has to fit the story, not the story fit the character.

So, if I have a fully developed character and then I work on the story, I often have to go back and change the personality of my character to make him/her fit.

We'll talk more about character later. **For now, if you have a character in mind, write his/her name in your note pad or computer file.**

Now we are going to develop or plot our story by looking at the building blocks that I mentioned. I will list them and then explain each one.

1. Inciting incident   2. Goal or Quest

3. Motivation   4. Primary action

5. Primary Conflict or Obstacles   6. Secondary obstacles

7. Point of no return   8. Climax

9. Resolution

Plotting: If followed, these BUILDING BLOCKS WILL GET A WRITER FROM BEGINNING TO END, SMOOTHLY. Let's look more closely at them.

1. Inciting incident:

A story should start with an inciting incident: Something out of the ordinary that happens to change your character's life. Many books spend the first few pages setting up the story: who the main characters are, where they live, what their life is like now etc, but this is not necessary and will bore your reader. This information should be woven into the story after you reveal the purpose of the story.

If you start with the inciting incident, you will hook the reader. This should be an event beyond the control of the protagonist, which turns things from average to exceptional. It can be huge or tiny, pleasant, or unpleasant, it may not even be recognised as significant at the time, but this is the point where the character's life changes.

For instance, for the plot for the first book in my Mystery of Nida Valley series, I wrote, 'Meg comes home from school and finds a note that says Amanda is missing.'

Write in the inciting incident for your story.

2. Goal or Quest:

The effect of the inciting incident is to generate the need for a goal or quest. **The quest or goal is important** – it's the whole reason for your story.

The protagonist now is forced to seek something or change something to get things back on track. When people hear the word quest, they assume you mean something like an adventure to get back the sacred chalice.

But a quest can be an emotional one. In romantic fiction, it could be to pursue the love of your life, in contemporary fiction it could be to pass an exam or get a degree, get a promotion or a new job, be chosen for the Olympics, beat a disease. Or in crime it could be to catch a killer, find a lost loved one or any number of things. The success of your narrative hangs on whether your reader thinks it is an interesting goal or quest. With a short story or a picture book, it can be simple, but it still must be life-changing or lifesaving.

With a novel, there is usually one huge life-changing or saving goal and several minor ones along the way that your hero has to achieve to reach the ultimate goal. This major goal should be very clear in your mind and must be clear to your reader early in the book.

Write in your character's major goal.

As you break down the story into scenes the other goals will become clear. The goal in the first chapter can be a simple one.

In a murder mystery in could be the search for a missing person. After the body is found, the major goal would be to catch the killer.

The major goal in Mystery of Nida Valley is to save from extinction the last remaining Australian megafauna that are in a hidden valley protected by a magic order.

Meg's first goal was to find Amanda. It is during this search that she learns about the major goal.

3. Motivation: Why does your main character want to achieve the goal?

Your character's MOTIVATION is the reason most people read on from this point. It must be strong and easy to relate to from a readers' point of view. If they relate to it, they will become emotionally involved and that will hook them.

In a short story or picture book, the main motivation will be apparent from the first page, but in a novel, it is common that the primary goal, and the motivation behind it, is not evident in the first chapter. But, right from page one there must be some goal and a motivation for achieving it.

In the Mystery of Nida Valley, Meg's motivation for the major goal is that she is to be the next leader of the magic order that protects the animals, and it is her job to save them.

Meg's motivation for her first goal is her friendship with Amanda.

Fill in your character's motivation to achieve the major goal. If you know what the first goal will be, put it in.

4. Primary Action:

The primary action is how your protagonists will achieve the major goal? This is a very important part of the story.

It can be as simple as a journey, as complex as fighting a battle, out-smarting an enemy, or it could be overcoming some inner-conflict like shyness or lack of confidence or even an illness. It might involve a criminal act or learning new skills. Whatever it is, it must be interesting, start at the beginning of the book, and continue to the climactic scene.

In the Mystery of Nida Valley, Meg's primary action to achieve her major goal is to develop her magic powers and fight the evil wizard who wants to exploit the animals for financial gain.

Meg's first action is to go to the haunted manor where Amanda went missing and look for her friend.

Fill in your character's primary action.

5. Primary Conflict or Obstacles: *Who or what blocks the way.*

A story without conflict is dull and boring; in fact, without conflict there is no story. It can be internal or external conflict. But it must be strong enough to block the way. Most people think of conflict as negative – a fight etc, but in a story, it can simply be a problem that needs to be solved or tension to resolve. It can be internal conflict – a feeling of not being good enough; not up to the challenge faced. It can also be much more of course, it could be a bad guy to defeat, a mountain to climb, or a rival to eliminate. It all depends on the genre of the story.

Remember, if the goal is easily achieved, the story is boring. So, the characters need to encounter real obstacles on their quest. To keep tension through the story and keep the reader guessing, the unexpected must happen. A poorly constructed incident is often predictable, foreseen ten pages back and boring when it occurs.

Fill in the primary conflict or obstacle.

Meg's primary conflict is the evil wizard, but many secondary conflicts occur before she finally faces him.

6. SECONDARY CONFLICTS OR OBSTACLES:

Before our protagonist reaches the final destination, the final confrontation, and the achievement of the Big Goal, we need a few escalating action scenes involving obstacles to raise the tension. Sometimes these only become evident as we plot the story further, or as we write.

In a short story or picture book, the secondary obstacles are minor and easily overcome, but they still must be there – to slowly increase the tension.

In a novel, they must be much more complex. To keep the tension mounting, they must be life threatening, or life changing, and escalating towards the climax. Once again, they can be physical or emotional.

Meg faces many obstacles in her quest. She is chased by the marsupial lion, trapped in a cave with a dragon, hunted by the evil wizard, and much more.

Fill in at least one of the secondary conflicts or obstacles if you know one.

7. Point of No Return: Before your hero reaches the climactic scene, we throw in a **point of no return**. This is when the protagonist realises that it is now 'do or die'. There is no going back. Up to this point, the character could have decided to pull out of the quest. The character may, at this point, be compulsive and driven, but feeling inadequate, and deluded and feel like giving up. He/she will of course carry on, but letting the reader see that your character is human and has self-doubts is important.

Something should happen that takes away the character's choice and makes him/her press on; make them realise that there is no turning back.

It can be a physical barrier behind him/her: a rockslide, a collapsed bridge, flooded river, snowstorm etc. In battle, it could be a large force of the enemy coming up behind. Or it could be an emotional one, a decision that his/her life must change, he/she must save a loved one in danger etc.

If the character comes to a stop, the story is over. If they are to continue the quest, they will have to change course, change tactic, and that means making a difficult decision to overcome this primary obstacle.

Once again, sometimes this point only becomes evident as we plot the story further or as we write.

If you know what will cause your character to hesitate, and what will make them change their mind, fill it in.

After Meg faced the many obstacles in her quest, she declared that she didn't want to be leader and decided to quit, but then she learnt that one of the animals was in danger and only her newly acquired magic skills could save it.

8. CLIMAX: After the point of no return, the final climactic scene is usually the overcoming of the major obstacle.

But it could be as the result of an accumulation of further events. This is where your hero will either win or lose. The critical choices he made on the journey come to a head in the climactic scene. It need not be spectacular, but it must be the high point of the drama in the story. In a physical or emotional journey, it is where the hero stands up against the thing he fears most and wins ... or loses. Whatever you decide. You are the God of your created world.

The climax must change the status of the character. If it does not result in a reversal of your protagonist's situation, which began with the inciting incident, then it begs the question if the climax was there solely for spectacle. If you have planted enough clues on the way, the reversal may have been expected, but you can always trot out a twist that changes your reader's expectation.

For the story to work well, we need to balance two things: unexpectedness and plausibility. Remember, it must be within the bounds of credibility. Even in fantasy or science fiction, credibility is expected.

This scene is virtually the reason for the story. If you don't have this firmly in your mind before you start, you can't plan the scenes that lead your character to this point.

Fill in the climactic scene

9. RESOLUTION:

The very last section is the resolution. This is sometimes a whole chapter. Sometimes it is just a couple of pages. This is where, in the murder mysteries, the killer reveals why he did it – or our hero tells us – and he is carted off to jail. In all stories, it is where we tie up any loose ends and trot out any twists. It's the 'then they rode off into the sunset and lived happily ever after' scene.

Fill in the resolution. Where does your character go from here?

But these building blocks don't just apply to the story, they should be used in every paragraph.

Let's look at a scene from my novel *The Mystery of Nida Valley*: Listen for the mix of action, description, and emotion that is needed to keep the reader engaged.

INCITING INCIDENT: An ear-piercing scream filled the air. Meg turned. Amanda stood frozen to the spot, looking up. Following her gaze, Meg yelped with fear. A snake like the one that had attacked Meg in the rainforest, coiled around the branch above Amanda's head.

RISING ACTION: It had been so close last time that Meg had no chance to take in its appearance. Now she gaped in wonder. It must be at least six metres long. Its striped, bright red body is as thick as a man's thigh. No wonder it was so strong, she thought. The rash on her arms prickled as she watched in horror. It uncoiled and dropped down towards Amanda.

POINT OF NO RETURN: 'Run, Amanda! Get away from it,' Meg shouted, edging away. But Amanda stood glued to the spot, shaking her head from side to side in fear, unable to move her legs.

CLIMAX: Jaiden quickly took out the stun gun and loaded a dart. Racing to Amanda's side, he pointed the gun at the snake and fired. But, although the dart sank deep into the flesh of the snake, it still kept coming towards them.

Meg rushed over and grabbed Amanda by the arm. 'Let's get out of here!' she cried. They pushed the buttons on their watches and landed at the base of the tree.

FALLING ACTION: The snake hissed fiercely in protest at its meal escaping once again. Legs trembling, the friends sank to the ground, and gasped to catch their breath.

RESOUTION: Meg looked up and sighed with relief; there was no sign of the snake following them. But their relief was short-lived. A shiver of warning passed through Meg's body, and she knelt to look around.

From the basic story outline you created you will be able to develop the plot for your story. The next book in this series will cover plotting in more detail.

This graph will help you with plotting the scenes along the way.

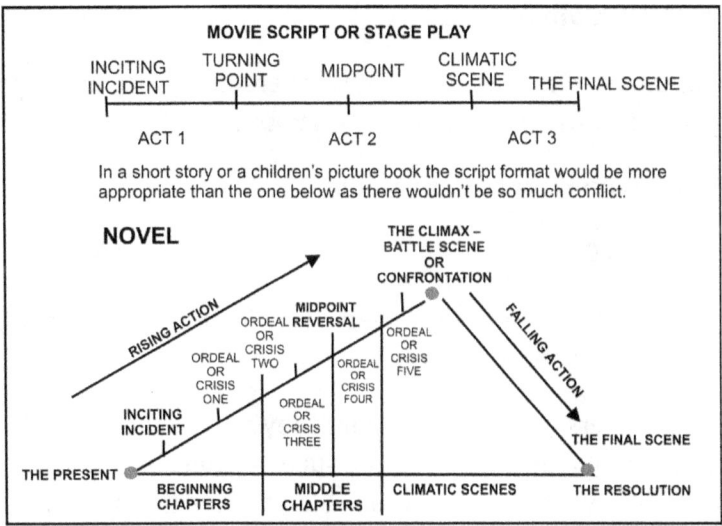

To make our story great, what else do we need to do?

DEVELOP STRONG CHARACTERS

We will work on those now. Let's start with our character. Now we know what our character has to do in the story we can make sure we give them the knowledge and attributes they need to achieve the outcome.

Chapter 2

DEVELOPING STRONG CHARACTERS

The best piece of advice on creating characters comes from a very famous author, Ernest Hemmingway. He said, 'Don't create characters, create people.'

Developing strong and believable characters that your reader either loves or hates – depending on your intention, is vital.

Let's start with our main character…

MAIN CHARACTER:

As I said earlier, every story needs a main character – this is the person whose story you will tell.

Good characters don't just happen; they are a deliberate blend of many elements arranged to produce a specific result in your particular story. They must fit the role you give them.

For instance, you wouldn't take a character who is covered in tattoos and swears with every second word and make him an English teacher in a girls' private school. It just wouldn't be believable. **Unless** there has been a problem (a cyclone, mass murder of teachers, etc.) and he is all they can get, of course. So, the character needs to fit the role to a certain extent.

How they live and where they live is important to the reader's perception of them. If they live in a wooden shack on the edge of town, we would assume they are poor.

And if they live in the most expensive house in town, we would assume they are rich. Now in a story with a twist, this is not always true, but we want our reader to believe what we show them until we are ready to reveal the truth. So, they must act like they belong.

You need to understand or research how people in the situation and era of your story would live, talk, and act. But don't stereotype them. Our personalities are developed early in our life from the teachings of our parents, and the lifestyle and environment we are raised in. So even if someone is born poor or rich there is no set personality type. There are many variables to the personality of your characters, no matter where they were raised. To portray them properly you need to know who they are, understand them, and be able to go into their head and **be them** while you write.

They also must be strong and interesting. When creating a character, we tend to use our own experiences, our understanding, values, and characteristics, but that is not enough. Do we really want all our characters to be just like us? Of course we don't, especially if we are writing more than one story.

There is nothing worse than reading a second novel from an author and realising that the character in the second one is just a clone of the one in the first book with a different name – or finding that all the characters in a novel are the same kind of people, good or bad.

Each character you develop must have a different personality or there is no inter-personal conflict, and the story is boring. So, you must portray your character's unique personality and motivations.

They must be people the reader can relate to. If your readers don't care about your main character and what happens to him or her, they won't read on. Many characters in books don't stand out, but a good author will have at least one in every story that jumps off the page.

Think about a character from a book who stayed in your mind after you closed the book. What made them so memorable? Do think you can develop your character to be that strong?

The most memorable character in a book I have read was Lisbeth, one of the main characters in Stieg Larsson's trilogy that began with *The Girl with the Dragon Tattoo.* Lisbeth had a strong personality disorder, and this disorder, like many, was directly related to her childhood and environment. But this made her fascinating, even though her behaviour was seemingly inconsistent at first. As I got into the story, I learnt about her background and started to understand her a little more, and my expectations of her actions in any given situation were not far wrong. Even though she broke many of the social rules we live by, and some laws, I developed a liking for her and cared what happened to her.

Many writers make the mistake of having characters who are too similar to each other and not well enough developed. Humans are not the same; we are multidimensional beings.

The best way to get to know your characters is to interview them. Now you are never going to use the answers in the story **directly**, but this knowledge will influence everything they do, say, and think. So, get to know all of your characters well before you start.

Here is a paragraph from *Butterfly* by award winning author Sonya Hartnett. Her character Plum is one of the strongest, most thought out characters in a YA story that I have read lately. This is at the beginning of the book.

'Plum is soon to turn fourteen, and one evening she stands in front of her mirror with her school dress around her ankles, her body reflected naked and distressing in the glass. If her reflection is true then she has gone about in public like this – thick black hair hugging her face like a sheenless scarf; these greasy cheeks with their evolving crop of scarlet lumps; this scruffy, hotly sunburned skin; these twin fleshy nubbins on her chest that are the worst things of all, worse than the specks of blackness blocking her pores – and nobody has informed her that she is hideous.'

What does this tell us about Plum? She hates herself. This is a good example of another topic I will cover in a later guide, 'Show, don't tell'. The author could have just said Plum hates herself and thinks she looks hideous, but it wouldn't have been as effective. So get to know your characters well and it will help you write like Sonya. If you interview your main character first, then it will also help you 'select' their friends and enemies.

You will find an interview at the end of the book that contains many questions that will help you understand and get to know your character. You may have to add a few of your own that relate specifically to your story and character.

But remember, this information is for your knowledge. You are not going to write a chapter on who your character is and how they got to this point in time. Many writers do. **This information is to help you know how your character will react in any situation you put them in.**

Some of it (the physical appearance and habits) you will feed into the story as you write. But most background facts will only be known by the reader *by the character's actions and reactions to situations in the story.*

To be a writer you also have to be an amateur psychologist. This book only touches on this complex subject.

Our Creative Writing Guide on characters examines the many personality types we meet and shows you how to portray them effectively. For crime and mystery writers, the character guide includes an examination of criminal types, and what drives them to commit crimes. It will help you learn how to develop strong characters.

Copy and fill in the character questionnaire at the back of the book on your main character. Use the questions that are relevant to your character and add any that you need.

Most stories have a few SECONDARY CHARACTERS

In a short story and a picture book, there can be just the one main protagonist, and the other people involved can be antagonists who are creating the conflict, but it is usual to give the hero a friend to help him or her.

In a novel, there are always a couple of sidekicks. And some people who could go either way and create a twist at the end.

Try not to create too many characters. It is hard for the reader to keep up with them. In a short story or picture book, the maximum recommended is three or four at the most – in a novel it can be more, but don't introduce them all at once. I would still keep the main protagonist friends to not more than three and the antagonists and his friends about the same. But there can be many more who are on the edge of the story – businesspeople, colleagues, teachers, family, parents, siblings, etc that drop into the story from time to time.

These secondary characters should help move the story forward. The interaction between them and the protagonist should add interest to the story.

You need to fill out an interview sheet on them too. Remember to make each one different in personality. This helps to create interesting moments in the story. In my fantasy series, *The Mystery of Nida Valley*, the best friend of the main character is the complete opposite of her. Our hero is brave and fearless and doesn't think anything of breaking rules if she feels she has a good reason. Her best friend is a stickler for the rules and a little timid. This creates conflict between them that adds to the entertainment and reality of the story. But as all characters should, they grow and learn from each other as the story progresses.

Fill in what you know about your secondary characters using the questions in the interview. Think each one through to make sure they have a different personality, but some have the same beliefs to give the character support, and some don't to create inter-personal conflict.

Now let's decide something else that is vital. What point of view will you use?

Chapter Three

ESTABLISHING POINT OF VIEW

Point of view is a technical device a writer uses to portray their story in what they consider the best way. Put simply it is: WHO SHOULD TELL THE STORY AND HOW THE STORY IS TO BE TOLD.

Before we decide on point of view let's look at what styles there are, and their individual advantages and disadvantages:

FIRST PERSON – Personal: This is where we write the whole book as if we are the main character. This POV is limited. You can only include details in the story that your character knows, sees, thinks, and hears. However, it is a powerfully emotive style if it is written well, as the reader at once identifies with the character. But all descriptions of the character are written from their POV so will be biased for or against. If you want another perspective on their appearance, you need to have another character tell us, by making a compliment, or a criticism. And if you are writing from the point of view of a small child, you would be limited to what they would understand, and be able to articulate at that age.

A perfect example of a strong **first-person personal** narrative is *Storm Glass* by Maria V Synder.

The first chapter starts:

'The hot air pressed against my face as I entered the glass factory. The heat and smell of burning coal surrounded me in a comforting embrace. I paused to breath in the thick air. The roar of the kilns sounded as sweet as my mother's voice.'

This tells us much about this character. What did you perceive from listening to that small passage? (I learnt that she loved her work environment and had a loving relationship with her mother.)

Use first person pronouns: I, me, my, etc.

Then there is **FIRST PERSON – Observer:** A story written from first person point of view doesn't have to be about the narrator, it can be an outside observer who is watching the main character and commenting on him. It is not his personal story he is relating. But, he can still only tell us what he knows, sees, thinks, and hears about the main character.

A good example is from *The Great Gatsby* by F. Scott Fitzgerald.

'Only Gatsby, the man who gives his name to this book, was exempt from my reaction – Gatsby, who represented everything for which I have an unaffected scorn. If personality is an unbroken series of successful gestures, then there was something gorgeous about him, some heightened sensitivity to the promises of life, as if he were related to one of those intricate machines that register earthquakes ten thousand miles away.'

So even though he is talking about someone else, he is speaking in the first person and telling us who the man is, and what he thinks of him.

FIRST PERSON – Memory: Is someone relating a memory of their past. But it is still limited to what they saw, heard, or were told. It uses the pronoun I, we, he, she.

This extract is from my YA novel *Restoring Destiny* and is from a chapter that is written in first person narrative from memory:

'I observed Yaholo greet your father with a short bow, and tell him that, as a gesture of peace, he would leave the giant guards outside the palace and proceed with just his personal guards. He requested time to rest and refresh before his meeting with King Marben. Baldasarre reluctantly agreed.

Ushering them to the visitors' quarters, I posted a guard outside the suite. I remember how Baldasarre, and the other advisors were pacing impatiently by the time the emissary emerged two hours later.'

So even in first person, there are three ways to approach this point of view.

SECOND PERSON POINT OF VIEW: Second person point of view is often used in non-fiction for giving directions, offering advice, or providing an explanation. It is also used in technical writing, advertising, songs, and speeches. This perspective allows the writer to make a connection with his or her audience by focusing on the reader.

In fiction, second person is used as a narrative voice similar to first person personal. It's a bit like talking to yourself – your subconscious mind addressing your conscious mind. It can also be a narrator relating to your main character their life story from the narrator's perspective.

This book is written in second person. But here is another example of an instructional script in second person:

'Making a sandcastle is a favourite project of beach-goers of all ages. Begin by digging up a large amount of sand (enough to fill at least six pails) and arranging it in a pile. Then, scoop the sand into your pail, patting it down and levelling it off at the rim as you do.

'You can now construct the towers of your castle by placing one pailful of sand after another face down on the area of the beach that you have staked out for yourself.'

As I said, it can be used effectively in fiction. This is the opening paragraph from Jay McInerney's *Bright Lights, Big City*: In this book, he is talking to himself.

'You are not the kind of guy who would be at a place like this in the morning. But here you are, and you cannot say that the terrain is entirely unfamiliar, although the details are fuzzy. You are at a nightclub talking to a girl with a shaved head.'

By using this writing style, the audience is drawn into the story immediately and becomes a part of the action.

Use second person pronouns: you, your, yours, etc.

THIRD PERSON LIMITED: Third person limited is closely related to **First Person** but vastly more open to insertions and observations from the author or narrator telling the story. **This is where the narrator limits the action and information the reader receives to what centers on or is known by** *the main character*. The story is written from that character's perspective, so nothing happens that does not happen in front of him.

The difference is that that the narrator can use any voice, any style of language or story structure. The narrative doesn't have to be written as if it is the character speaking.

The narrator can make comments on the main characters appearance like, 'His face turned purple with rage'. In first person, the main character would have to say, 'I felt the heat rising to my face and knew my rage must be showing'.

The following example is from *Time of Trial* by Michael Pryor:

'Caroline Hepburn was waiting for him at the gate. She was dressed in a long skirt and blouse, fresh and white. The blouse was fastened at her neck with an onyx brooch. Her hair was pinned, or layered, or constrained in some way that Aubrey admired but would never have ventured an opinion on exactly how it was done. Caroline's hair had been the cause of much thought on Aubrey's part.'

So you can see that even though this is limited to the Main Character's POV, the author has more freedom to comment on what is happening to our main character. He is also privy to his inner thoughts and feelings. This is a very common style. I use this style for my fantasy series, *The Mystery of Nida Valley*.

Here is a short passage:

'She waved goodbye to Charles and hurried to the gate that led to the side garden. Instinct tapped her on the shoulder and told her someone was nearby. The hairs on the back of her neck stood on end. As she turned to check behind her, out of the corner of her eye, she saw a figure move. She whirled around in time to see Grundymere charging towards her. Meg yelped with fear and pushed the travel button on her watch. Just as he reached her, she vanished.'

THIRD PERSON OMNISCIENT: A major point of view to consider is one of the most prevalent and certainly an immediate choice for many storytellers. The omniscient point of view is defined as the narrator of the story having access to any information past or present, stated or silent, enacted or thought, *relative to any character in the story*.

The narrator may include information about the thoughts and feelings of more than one character, and may also present the character's outward appearance, actions, and dialogue - it lets you see all characters through many people's eyes.

The narrator can, essentially, report anything at all, internal or external, hence the term omniscient or all knowing.

It also allows the reader to know things that relate to your main character but are not known by him. They may be known by one other character or only the narrator. Hence, the reader knows more than the main character and wonders what will happen when she/he finds out. This is a great suspense builder, and such secrets can be an important part of the character's journey.

You see it used a lot in horror movies where the audience sees the bad guy sneaking up on the hero, but he isn't aware he is there. You sit on the edge of your seat saying, "No, don't open the door!" This works just as well in books.

There are many ways to use this point of view. The best is to limit the change of point of view to different chapters.

I have used the omniscient point of view for my YA novel *Restoring Destiny*. Right from the first chapter, the reader knows that one of the main characters' friends is in fact plotting against them. This increases the tension as the reader wonders if they or their mentor will discover this in time to stop her.

It is also written from four character's POV. If you use this point of view, try to limit it to about three or four characters, and try not to head hop too much on each page. Too many is too confusing.

The following extract is from my novel:

'They all settled down for the night, but no-one got much sleep. Kanda and Rais were worried about their guardians.

Palesa could not get the image of Leopold out of her head. She had a vague feeling of having known him before. Something about him stirred a curious feeling in her, one she had never felt before; a need to protect and defend him. *I wonder if he used to live in the palace. Maybe we were friends.*

Briador lay there trying to plan the twins' magic lessons. The worry that they would not be fully prepared when they arrived at the city was paramount in his mind. If Briador knew what Palesa was planning, he would realise he had a bigger worry.'

This last foreshadowing comment increases the tension.

I have seen the OMNISCIENT point of view used in a more head hopping and confusing style, as in this paragraph:

'The girl was watching carefully, her gaze fixed on the corner. She had seen him somewhere – but where? To her dismay, the man turned towards her. He moved; he saw her. He noticed she was looking at him; *She is so beautiful,* he thought to himself, but didn't change his expression at all. Instead, he walked towards the door; without looking directly at her. His friend, Cottlestone looked up from the parlor door; his face turned pale; he nearly fainted. "It's the girl from the marketplace!" he hissed to Hedges, who was thinking about the weather.'

To me that is way too much head-hopping.

It is probably the easiest style to use as it can be used in many ways, and you can choose how it will best suit your story. I would avoid head hopping to four characters in one short paragraph, as in the one above.

OBJECTIVE: This POV is defined as 'the fly on the wall' who simply notes what he sees and hears, without intrusion or interpretation.

The observer isn't involved in the action of the scene; instead, he's just watching and listening like a video camera.

The objective point of view is characterised by showing the audience only what the characters look like, say, or do. The audience must interpret the actions and words of the character directly, as opposed to being told by a narrator or protagonist how the characters feel about what is happening to them. It's a more commentary style of writing, recording events without feeling, as a camera would do.

Here is an extract from the novel *Popular Mechanics* by Raymond Carver: 'Early that day the weather turned, and the snow was melting into dirty water. Streaks of it ran down from the little shoulder-high window that faced the backyard. Cars sloshed by on the street outside, where it was getting dark. But it was getting dark inside too. He was in his bedroom pushing clothes into a suitcase when she came to the door.

"I'm glad you're leaving! I'm glad you're leaving!" she said. "Do you hear?"

He kept on putting his things into the suitcase.'

The point of view in this story is so distant and impersonal that it might seem easy for the reader to stay removed from the emotion and conflicts in the story. But as the story unfolds, you get just as involved in the emotion as you would in any other style of writing. The clever dialogue portrays the emotion, and the reader imagines the rest.

To help you understand point of view, try writing the extract from Raymond Carver in the different points of view covered. Then choose the point of view you think will suit your story. After you have written the first couple of paragraphs, try writing them in different POVs to see which one suits.

Chapter Four

CREATING THE BEST SETTING

Setting is the time, place, and mood in which a story takes place. It is often the heart of the narrative. For the reader to be able to relate to the story, you must identify those details in your story that establish the time, place, and the overall mood of the story.

If you want to set it in a particular country, era or city, research is necessary to ensure your information is correct. For instance, if it is a period setting, you would need to know the style of clothes worn, the kind of vehicles available at that time, and many minor details, down to what kind of watches, electrical appliances etc they had. There is so much research needed for that genre of story. That is why I like fantasy – I can make my setting anything I want it to be.

But setting also helps create the mood of the story and increases the conflict. Bad weather, a mountain to climb, etc all add to the conflict. But for readers to totally engage with your story you have to paint word pictures that describe the scene when they arrive at a different place.

For an example of setting used purely to establish mood, here is an extract from my book *The Mystery of Nida Valley*: Meg has discovered that her best friend has gone missing at the local historic manor. She sets out to find her.

'Distant thunder rolled like the sound of empty drums on a concrete floor, as the dark clouds of a late-afternoon storm covered the sky. Meg leaned her bike on the stone fence and strode through the gates, ignoring the goosebumps crawling up her arms. The crunch of her sneakers on the loose gravel driveway announced her presence and she peered around nervously. A gusty wind blew eerily through the tall pines that lined the drive; their shadows swaying and dancing like ghosts at a Halloween party. The dark stone manor towered menacingly as she approached. According to rumour, it is haunted.'

This kind of passage sets the mood for the rest of the scene. It increases the tension. Already we know that something strange is going to happen. And we read on, wanting to find out what it is. Of course, the mood of the story will change through the story. So, your description of surroundings will change to suit the mood.

Many writers over-describe the setting and scenery. While a well described setting will help the reader, too much information bogs the story down and slows the pace.

When you are describing the setting, CREATE WORD PICTURES USING ALL OF YOUR SENSES:

One of the best ways to turn bland, lifeless setting descriptions into interesting, poetic writing is by adding details. When you're writing, close your eyes and imagine the scene. This way you 'see' the small details that make your writing interesting and give your reader a true feeling for where your character is and what is happening. Most writers are visual people, and each scene is usually described from a visual perspective, but you can add more interest if you use all of your senses. This helps to transport the reader to the place.

What do your characters **HEAR – TASTE – SEE – SMELL – FEEL (physically and emotionally)**

Example: I opened the curtains and looked out the window. It was raining out there now.

Rewritten: 'I opened the curtains to allow the last glimmer of light to enter. The sky outside had sunk into a deep depression. Its grey pallor tugged at my mood trying to draw me into its melancholy. Nature's tears streaked the window as the wind rattled it in its frame. Even the air was thick with the scent of rain and damp. I quickly closed out the dismal scene and turned on the light. I hugged my favourite sky-blue cushion and wondered if the sun would ever shine again.'

This transports the reader not only to the scene, but into the emotion of the character.

In my YA novel, *Restoring Destiny,* I have used the theme of the sun and moon competing for the right to light the sky. Here are a couple of paragraphs of the ways I said it was sunset or sunrise.

What I could have said: He stood and watched the sunrise over the water.

The paragraph from the novel: 'He breathed the fresh salty air that blew gently from the sea and licked the tang of the salt from his lips. Gulls called to each other as they flew lazy circles in the morning sky. Entranced, he watched the day begin. The ocean's surface rippled as if the golden globe rising from it was shaking large drops of water from its night cloak. Its glow touched the top of the ripples and created a shimmering staircase leading to the morning sky. The moon retreated, as if turning its back on the sun's blinding light.'

What I could have said: She woke with a start and broodingly watched the sunset.

The paragraph from the novel: 'She woke with a start. The day was almost over. The scent of the flowering bush beside her filled the air, as she stared broodingly at the distant mountains that divided Nevaah from Gantis. The buzzing of the bees gathering nectar from its blooms broke the silence that surrounded her. Behind the mountains, the sun had painted the sky the colour of fire to signal its time of rest. She watched as it took a final bow to kiss the top of the rise, before slipping away behind it, handing the moon the duty of lighting their way.'

Write in the setting you will use in your story. Include Year – Season – Place – Mood.

So now that we have covered what you need to build your story where do you start?

Start at an action scene.

Always start your story at a dramatic point. The inciting incident. As I said earlier, many people spend the first chapter TELLING the reader about the protagonist – their background, the way they look, their present circumstances, and then lead slowly into the problem that is the crux of the story. By the end of the first two pages, you have lost the reader.

The things we have covered are the building blocks of a story. In my next book, Plotting and Waking Your Imagination, we will cover how to expand what we have developed into a story that will make the readers want to stay reading until the end.

CHARACTER QUESTIONAIRE:

This questionnaire is for all major characters in your story. But start with the main character. You can see that by answering these questions, you are building the personality of your characters. The first question you need to answer are these:

1. What is your character's role in your story?
2. What physical attributes will they need for that role?
3. What emotional attributes will they need for that role?
4. What skills will they need for that role?

The answers to those 4 questions will influence the answers to the following ones.

Now ask your characters these questions: This questionnaire should be filled in with the role the character has in your story in mind. Some question will only be relevant to certain genres and stories. You can add any other questions you think you need.

What is your name? How old are you? How tall? What is your build? What colour are your eyes, hair, skin?

Are you: Confident, Shy, Afraid, Weak, Strong, Clever, Dumb Average, Other?

Do you have a bad habit?

What are the things you like most about yourself?

What are the things you like least about yourself?

Describe how you think others see you?

Do you have any stand-out personal habits or way you dress?

Where were you raised? How would you describe your childhood?

What do/did your parents do for a living?

What were your parents like? Strict, Loving, Uncaring, Violent, other? What was/is your favourite class at school?

What are some experiences from your childhood that have affected the sort of person you are now?

Where do you now live? What is your job? Do you like it?

Are you rich, poor, or in-between?

Are you married/in a relationship? Is your relationship a happy one? If not, why?

Do you have any special belief systems?

What are your talents and skills? Do any of these talents or skills have a downside?

Do you have any mannerisms or speech quirks?

How many siblings do you have? What are your siblings' most annoying traits? What do you like about your siblings?

Who is your best friend? What are he/her best traits?

What do you look for in a friend? What do you look for in a partner?

If you had a secret, to whom would you tell it?

Of what are you afraid? What makes you happy?

What is your favourite food? What food makes you want to puke?

Who is your worst enemy? Why is he your enemy?

How do you feel about discipline?

Are you someone who fits in with society or someone who fights it?

How would you spend a typical day?

What do you want more than anything in the world?

www.ingramcontent.com/pod-product-compliance
Lightning Source LLC
Chambersburg PA
CBHW051949160426
43198CB00013B/2369